Mediumship – Raising the Standards

Exercise Book 1

By

Tim Abbott

Con-Psy Publications

First Edition

© Tim Abbott
2014

Published by
CON-PSY PUBLICATIONS
P.O. BOX 14,
GREENFORD,
MIDDLESEX, UB6 0UF.

ISBN 978 1 898680 65 9

Thanks go to my family that have supported me throughout the development of my mediumship. Special thanks to

Beckie and Robin

who helped me format this book.

I would also like to thank all of the many students I have taught throughout my years of teaching. It's because of you I had the inspiration to write this book.

Contents

Chapter One

Getting To Know Me

I was born in Saffron Walden in August 1960. Saffron Walden is a small town in Essex, very closely located to the Arthur Findlay College. Unfortunately, I was born into a very dysfunctional family and by the age of 4, along with three of my siblings, I was put into a children's home where I stayed until I was 11 years old. It was during this period that I first became aware of the Spirit World.

I believe my first mediumistical experience was at the age of 7. At the age of 11, I was reunited with my mother, then living in Fulham, Central London, where she introduced me to Spiritualism. At the age of 19, after many experiences with the Spirit World, I decided to study Spiritualism and develop my mediumship. Very quickly it was clear to me that I was not suited to circle work, so under the guidance of the Spirit World I would sit at home each day for about an hour meditating. During these sessions individuals would come to me from the Spirit World giving me many different experiences with teaching and developing my mediumship in mind. This closely bonded the relationship I had formed with the Spirit World during this time and would keep me in good stead in the future with the support and exercises the Spirit World would offer me in years to come when I had developed as a teacher of mediumship.

I started studying at the Arthur Findlay College in 1994 and within a short period of time I was encouraged to enrol on the Teacher Training Scheme. This involved a 3 year practical training programme in which I developed my knowledge and practicality of teaching. There was one small problem however, I'm dyslexic, but with the encouragement of the Spirit World and being inspired by my guides with exercises to aid my teaching, I passed with flying colours and immediately I was fortunate enough to secure teaching work at the college. This accelerated into invitations to teach in many different countries around the world.

All this time the Spirit World continued and still continue to offer me different teaching exercises, of which some I offer to you within this book. At this time I currently am a course organiser at the Arthur Findlay College where I run the course *'MEDIUMSHIP - RAISING THE STANDARDS,'* which has become so much in demand that it is now a stand-alone course, which means we have the use of the whole college because of the number of students this course caters for.

I have also recently achieved two diplomas within my mediumship, one for teaching and one for demonstrating. I also currently teach in eight different counties throughout the world. I am a great believer that, immaterial to any impediments an individual may have when in the company of Spirit for the purpose of mediumship, there are no limitations to the standard and the quality that we can achieve within our mediumship and I hope that the exercises in this book give you the same potential as the Spirit World has offered to me.

Chapter Two

How I Got Into Mediumship

"The Hangman Returns"

Whilst I continued to have regular experiences with the Spirit World as a young man, I really had no interest in becoming a working medium. However, one event would change all of this. I was in my early 20s and I was working for a building firm in Fulham, London when we were contracted to refurbish a top floor flat in the neighbouring borough of Hammersmith. The electrician and myself arrived at the property early on a Monday morning only to find that sadly, during the weekend, a man had broken into the flat and taken his own life by hanging himself.

Later on we would discover that he was involved in a murder case and was awaiting sentencing at the Old Bailey that very Monday morning. After my colleague and I discovered the body, I needed to take control of the situation, which involved comforting my colleague, who had become very emotional and also I was required to inform and wait for the police. Due to the traumatic events of the day, I decided to retire to the comfort of my local pub.

After several weeks - and having put the event behind me - in the early hours of one morning I was awoken from my sleep with an awareness of the presence of a man in my bedroom. After opening my eyes and sitting up in my bed, I found myself looking at the spirit of the very man who had hanged himself standing at the foot of my bed, mouthing something. Although I was unable to hear his words, I had a knowing that he was apologising for the way that I had found his hanging body.

Over a period of two weeks this gentleman appeared three times to me. With concern, I seeked the advice of a medium - Terry Evans. It was through Terry's support and guidance that I was introduced to mediumship. Whilst he put my fear to rest, he also saw the potential within me and invited me to his circle (class for mediumship), which was held at Balham Spiritualist Church in London.

The very first time I attended the circle Terry asked me to come to the front of the group and tell my story. In reply to his request I said: "Ooh No, I've only come to thank you, I'm not interested in this mediumship malarkey." After some persuasion and some reluctance I stepped up to the front of the group and with Terry's support found myself giving my first ever clairvoyant message. I was drawn to one of the ladies within the group and explained to her that I could see in my mind a young man in an army uniform and how he kept taking me to an isolated house on a hill, following which he kept showing me flames from a fire.

Terry enquired with the lady as to whether she could understand the information I was relaying to her as this was a lady that I'd never met before. She explained that when her only son was on leave from the army he was killed in a house fire in their family home, which was an isolated house on Hill Way. At the end of the evening Terry spoke to me privately, explaining to me that I had a gift of mediumship and if I wished, he would help me to develop it.

I attended Terry's circle a further six times. After this, whilst very grateful for Terry's input, I came to the conclusion that his circle was not really for me. By now I had embraced the desire to develop my mediumship, so I quickly found an alternative circle in which to study. Sadly after approximately six weeks this also seemed not to be the circle for me, so I found yet another and the same thing happened again. After approximately six weeks it seemed as if the people within the circle were talking a completely different language to me. After the last visit to the third circle I returned home frustrated, stood in my front room and shouted out loud, directing my voice to the ceiling: "I can't do this, I can't find anybody to teach me". To my amazement I heard objectively: "We will teach you if you like" - a voice coming from the Spirit World.

The voices directed me to sit in a meditational state once a day, each time for approximately an hour. Within that timeframe individuals would come from the Spirit World to give me different experiences and exercises and little did I know at the time that this was developing my mediumship. I sat each day for two years, never missing a day. I had found my circle, somebody to teach me. Bizarrely, my tutor was a dead man, my fellow circle members were dead people, but the bond and blending that I had within those two years would be the foundation of my mediumship for years to come.

Chapter Three

A Positive
Approach

It is important to accept that within mental mediumship, psychology plays a big role and during the practice of mediumship a positive approach is vital. For example, if a student was to say to him or herself: "I never see the spirit communicator!" the probability is that they never will, simply because they are mentally accepting those limitations within their sensitivity and awareness.

If we look at evidence offered up by a medium during the practice of mediumship, it is important that the medium takes on the mental approach that the definition of evidence is an expression of the intelligence of Spirit and during the act of mediumship we must be seeking to achieve this very thing.

If the Spirit World is a world of intelligence, the individuals communicating from the Spirit World will be interacting with the medium through their logic, their reasoning, their education and their purpose. Whilst the medium may be interacting with the communicator, it is important that the communicator is allowed to direct the subject matter and direction that the sitting or demonstration takes.

As mediums, we are ambassadors for the Spirit World. Any limitations within our mediumship are sadly those that we choose to own. We must remember at all times during the act of mediumship that it is our duty through our mediumship to express the intelligence, the presence and the evidence of the Spirit World.

Therefore, if you can approach your relationship and interaction with those individuals who choose to interact with you from the Spirit World as of much as a natural process as possible, you will find that you will minimise the limitations within the relationship. You would not have any limitations within the interaction between you and your loved ones so, therefore, why have any limitations between you and your clients' loved ones?

So let's have a look at the process of mediumship so we can understand the importance and the value of the exercises offered up in this book.

Chapter
Four

The Natural Process Of Mental Mediumship

It is important that we understand the process
through which the practice of mediumship comes about.

Sensitivity

and

Awareness

can bring about

The possibilities of Psychic Experiences

and in harmony with your

Spiritual Attunement

This can bring about

The potential for the act of mediumship

Through the development of an individual's sensitivity (i.e. psychic ability) and the inclusion of the presence of Spirit, the individual has the potential to put into practice the art of mediumship.
The spirit communicator will express their presence, personality and thoughts as energy to the medium, who then perceives the energy through their Clairvoyant, Clairaudient and Clairsentient abilities (i.e. psychic abilities).

Only when the medium expresses his or her experiences of spirit comes about the

Practice of Mediumship

Sensitivity

Have you noticed how a mushroom, through its sensitivity, will react to the morning dew? It becomes more open within its structure and have you been aware of how a flower, through its sensitivity, reacts to the rain?

Each and every one of us is sensitive. How we use that sensitivity differs from person to person. Through exercises and regular development, students who are studying their psychic and mediumistical abilities come to accept and indeed work with and through their sensitivity. If we look at the human aura:

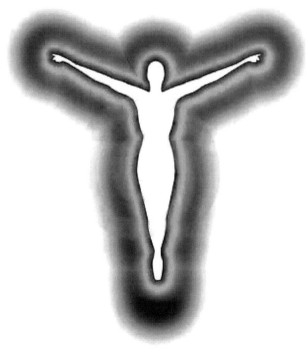

From the early 1940s, for many years, the Russian husband and wife team, Semyon and Valentina Kirlian, (Kirlian photography) did in depth research on the auric field, discovering that plants, animals and indeed human beings have an auric field.

This is an electromagnetic energy field which is sensitive to other energies that either blend or impinge upon it. In my understanding the auric field is made up of many different ingredients of energy, which include **Mental** energy, that is to say that some of the energy created through our thought process will abide within the auric field. Added to this is **Physical** energy, that is to say that some of the energy created through our physical body will abide within the auric field, **Emotional** energy, that is to say some of the energy created within our emotions will abide within the auric field and also **Spiritual** energy, that is to say some of the energy emanating from our own incarnate spirit will abide within the auric field.

These different energies will fluctuate and change from time to time according to the natural changes and experiences that come within an individual's life. For example, if an individual suffered a bereavement through the loss of a loved one, this would affect their emotional energy and therefore change the level of emotional energy within the auric field.

With this understanding of the auric field we have to remember that the Spirit World is both a world of intelligence and a world of energy, therefore when an individual steps forward from the Spirit World to communicate through an individual's mediumship, there is what is termed "a blending of energies" i.e. auric fields between both the medium and the communicator. This blending will bring about a change or an effect upon the auric field and the *Sensitivity* of the medium.

Awareness

Awareness is an activity of the medium's mind or consciousness, acknowledging, yet not interfering, with the affect and changes to the sensitivity of the medium due to the blending of spiritual energy (possibly an individual from the Spirit World). Through extensive development the student of mediumship learns not to change the effect to his or her sensitivity with their own thoughts, logic or conclusion, yet simply be aware of the changes within their own sensitivity. This can come about through *The Possibilities of psychic experiences*.

Although there are several, the three main senses that can come about through the psychic abilities of either the psychic or medium are those known as:

CLAIRVOYANCE = to clearly see the spiritual energy.

CLAIRSENTIENCE = to clearly sense the spiritual energy.

CLAIRAUDIENCE = to clearly hear the spiritual energy.

It is believed that these phrases were introduced by the Marquis de Fuysegur in the eighteenth century. If we take, for example, a medium, when interacting with an individual from the Spirit World, the effect the individual has upon the medium's sensitivity is first experienced through the auric field. This can then be perceived through the psychic senses. For example, the medium may see the presence of the spirit communicator, sense the presence of the communicator, or hear the presence of the communicator.

Spiritual Attunement

It is understood that the Spirit World shares the same space as we do within our own physical existence; however, the frequency of the energy in which the Spirit World exists, moves at a different pace to the frequency of energy that we exist within.

It is understood that the frequency of energy within the Spirit World is both finer and faster of that of ours and this is why individuals who have not developed their mediumistical abilities would not normally be aware of that finer vibration (the Spirit World). Through different exercises and therefore development of one's sensitivity, a medium develops the ability to attune (Spiritual Attunement) to the Spirit World.

Trained mediums have developed the ability to take their awareness to that finer vibration that exists as part of the Spirit World.

The potential for the act of mediumship

The definition of mediumship is to mediate. During the act of mediumship, an individual relays to a recipient what he or she is aware of through their Sensitivity and Psychic senses whilst in the company of an individual from the Spirit World and through the intelligence or thought process of that individual and what it is they wish to relay to the said client. It is only when the medium is expressing the thoughts of the communicator that we can define the act of mediumship.

If we keep in mind the process of mediumship, there are various opinions on the question as to whether mediums are born or developed. Whilst I accept mediums are probably born with a potential, that potential needs to be developed into an ability.

If we take, for example, the famous violinist Nigel Kennedy, whilst he showed great musical potential as a young boy, he still attended and studied at the Yehudi Menuhin School of Music then later at the Juilliard School in New York, fine tuning his musical ability, turning it from a potential into a wonderful ability.

Mediumship is no different; I would always recommend students of mediumship find a development circle under the guidance of a good tutor. Each time we are in the company of Spirit, be it for the sake of an exercise or simply for the beauty of the company of Spirit, we are both exercising and strengthening (developing) our Sensitivity, Awareness, Psychic Abilities and The Art of Mediumship.

Whilst I am sure the Spirit World may have something to say about the type of medium we may become, how far we take our mediumship is our responsibility. It is important that we feed and nurture our potential. We feed our potential through mediumistical exercises and we nurture our potential by simply being in the company of Spirit.

So now we hopefully can see the value of different exercises and how they can improve and strengthen both our relationship with the Spirit World and our mediumship. The exercises within this book are suitable for mental mediumship (clairvoyant mediumship).

Through partaking in these exercises, our goal is to heighten the students' sensitivity. Added to this, the strengthening of their awareness, the understanding of their own psychic abilities and the ability to be - and stay - within the company of Spirit, as well as a professional approach to the presentation and delivery of their mediumship.

Chapter Five

Exercises For Beginners

Exercise 1

When starting the journey of mediumistical development it is important that the student, firstly, familiarises him or herself with their own sensitivity.

Exercise 1 offers the student to do just that. Either as part of a group or on your own, go into the quiet, i.e. relax the physical body and allow the thoughts within the consciousness to be passive and few preferably this can be done whilst sitting in an upright chair and accepting within the mind from the outset that you will have the company of an individual from the Spirit World.

After approximately 1 minute of stilling yourself then take your attention to your breath; you don't need to change the breath at all, just simply observe it again for about a minute. During the minute be aware of how you feel, for example, you may feel a temperature change within your body, you may see different colours within your mind's eye or you may be aware of a shift within your emotions (these are all normal experiences that come about when your sensitivity is heightened).

After the minute has lapsed I would like you to invite an individual from the Spirit World to come and join you, to be in your company (blend with you). Take your awareness away from the breath and allow yourself to perceive the individual from the

Spirit World as they step forward and simply be in their company for no other purpose than for being in their company.

After approximately 1 minute of having the company of your visitor from the Spirit World, once again become aware of how you feel and compare how you feel when having the company of an individual from the Spirit World and when you were in the company of simply your own breath.

Then, thank your visitor and invite him or her to return back to the Spirit World taking your awareness back to your breath, once again for approximately 1 minute. Repeat this process three times with the same individual from the Spirit World.

This will allow you to explore and accept how it feels when you have the company and indeed when you do not have the company of an individual from the Spirit World. If in a group, after the exercise, discuss your findings.

This exercise will encourage your sensitivity to become heightened and for your awareness of that sensitivity to be both structured and disciplined.

Exercise 2

The following exercise is best practised in pairs. Decide between the two students which one of you will work first.

The student working first, like with any exercise, will need to give themselves time to settle down, accepting that within this period of settling down that their sensitivity will become heightened.

The student working will take their awareness to their fellow student, accepting in their mind that whilst doing this they will perceive the auric field of their fellow student (accepting that you may see, hear or sense your partner's auric field). On doing so you will become aware of the energy within your partner's auric field.

Part of how you will perceive the energy will be as colour. I would like you to focus on one particular colour, remembering that this colour is part of your partner's presence. I would like you to verbalise a character reading to your partner based around that one colour.

The aspects of your partner I would like you to cover are their mental state, physical state, emotional and spiritual state, so, for example, if you are feeling from your partner the colour red, cover what the colour red says about your partner's mental state, followed by their physical state followed by their emotional and finally spiritual state.

Do try and cover all four aspects from one colour. The exercise should take approximately 15 minutes and on completion you can discuss your findings with your partner and then change roles.

The benefits of this exercise are that you are encouraging depth within your statements which will, further on in your development, encourage depth within your mediumship.

Exercise 3

The following exercise has been designed to heighten your sensitivity and awareness and to be able to recognise shifts and changes within the energy, which will be perceived through your sensitivity and acknowledged through your awareness:

This exercise is suitable for pairs or groups of up to approximately six students. You will need a blindfold, preferably the type of blindfold used by people on planes for sleeping. You will also require four natural objects, for example, a crystal approximately the size of a fist, a flower, preferably in bloom, an apple and a potato (a fruit and a vegetable).

Clear a table and place the four objects in a row on the table about 6 inches apart from each other. Between yourselves decide which student is going to work first (chairs can be used if required).

Blindfold the student who is working and then nominate a spokesperson within the group; the spokesperson will need to stand or sit on the opposite side of the table of which the student is working.

Firstly, allow the student who is working a minute to settle themselves down both mentally and physically, which will bring about the desired effect of heightening the senses, after which the spokesperson will take hold of one of the working student's hands and place it over the first of the four objects on the table leaving a gap between the hand and the object of about 3 to 4 inches.

The spokesperson will make the simple statement: "Your hand is above............," stating what object is beneath, giving the student approximately a minute to become aware of the energy emanating from the object.

After this, the student will verbalise how the energy feels or affects them. This process will be repeated with each object on the table. The spokesperson can direct the student to move their hand away from the table and relax, followed by the spokesperson removing one of the objects from the table, ensuring that the student is unaware of which object has been removed (it is important that the object is moved a far distance away from the table).

After a further minute the spokesperson once again will take hold and control of the student's hand. Placing the student's hand once again over the first object, the spokesperson will simply say: "This is where the crystal is or was," giving the student a minute to attune themselves once again to the energy of the object or not as the case may be.

This will be repeated four times covering the three remaining objects and including the space from where one object has been removed. The goal of the exercise is for the student who is working to voice where he or she senses the energy has diminished (which object has been removed).

This exercise can be repeated according to how many students are in the group. It is important for the student to remain blindfolded throughout the duration of the exercise.

Exercise 4

It is important when working with an individual from the Spirit World that the student interacts with the communicator (like within any relationship or interaction between two people when both have an input, the relationship or interaction is enriched).

The following exercise is suitable to be carried out in pairs (one-to-one sitting). As always, the student who is working first must give themselves time to settle down, which will allow their sensitivity to become heightened and will allow them to attune to the Spirit World.

Invite an individual from the Spirit World to join you. On achieving the company of an individual from the Spirit World, describe the individual to your recipient, then invite the spirit communicator to give you some information about themselves (remember you may see, hear or feel this information).

After the communicator has expressed this further information about themselves, through the power of their mind, ask a question to the communicator based on what they have just expressed to you (encouraging the communicator to give you more depth on the intial statement they had made).

Remember, you will perceive the answer from your communicator through either seeing, hearing or feeling. For example, Grandad from the Spirit World expresses to the student that he died of a chest condition. The student may, through the power of their mediumship, ask Grandad what type of chest condition it was, i.e. heart, lungs or possibly even cancer.

The student will then allow their mind to be still, which will then allow them to perceive the answer offered from Grandad in the Spirit World. The student will then verbalise the statement or story from Grandad to the recipient in its fullest sense.

I would suggest that the student tries this question-and-answer approach with the spirit communicator at least twice during the one-to-one sitting which should take approximately 10 to 15 minutes.

After the sitting is complete both students can discuss their findings and then change roles and repeat the exercise.

Remember this exercise is not geared around evidence but around the relationship and interaction the student has with the spirit communicator.

Exercise 5

If we look at a story within a newspaper, an email sent through a computer and a handwritten letter, they will all have a structure - a beginning, a middle and an end. Any form of mediumship, be it from the platform or of a one-to-one nature, is best expressed with structure (format) and when it does hold a structure, it gives it value, simply through presentation. Throughout my years of development, different tutors would show me different structures of how to deliver a message, some of which were very complicated.

There should be nothing complicated about mediumship. The following exercise is designed to give a simple and natural, yet structured, format to the delivery of your mediumship. This exercise can take the format of either a one-to-one sitting or delivered through platform work. If we look at the one-to-one sitting, based on a 15 minute sitting, the student who is working first will structure the sitting as follows:

After completing the exercise discuss your findings and change roles. I would suggest that as part of your development you carry out this exercise approximately six times over a period of a few weeks, which will allow you to take on board the format suggested, after which I would suggest you discard the handout and allow the format to be expressed naturally.

Messages Made Natural

To allow the interaction between the medium and the Spirit World to become more natural, we should allow the communicator to relay information they wish to express rather than that which the medium demands.

1. **Introduce the spirit communicator** *(Male or female).*
2. **Give evidence relating to a pastime, hobby or lifestyle that the communicator was passionate or dedicated to, occasionally including further information personal to the communicator** *(plus any additional evidence that the Spirit World wish to express).*
3. **Allow the evidence to inspire you with the reason for coming** *(The message).*
4. **How the communicator, not the medium, wishes to bring the communication to a close** *(Goodbye).*

As a medium, when working with a natural structure to your message, you will find it easier for both the World of Spirit, you and the recipient to understand the information being relayed by the communicator.

The above is a handout I use within my own courses; I would recommend that the student has a copy of it to hand whilst working if they need it to refer to.

Exercise 6

I have the greatest respect for those people who choose only to work on the psychic level, i.e. psychics. However, it is important for those students of mediumship to know when they are working indeed on the psychic level or mediumistical level with the Spirit World, i.e. discarnate spirit.

Spiritual science tells us that if you are working either psychically or mediumistically that you are working with spiritual energy; however, the frequency of both energies are moving at a different pace, therefore the way psychic energy would affect your sensitivity when working and perceiving it would be different to mediumistical discarnate energy.

The following exercise is designed to highlight, for the student, the difference. This exercise is suited for one-to-one sittings. I would suggest that the sitting lasts for approximately 15 minutes, during which the student should have established a close blend with the communicator and that is to say that the recipient knows who the communicator is.

As the student working delivers a statement from the spirit communicator, of which the recipient can accept, I would like the student to pause, not looking for any more evidence yet holding onto the company of the spirit communicator.

At this point, the student working should explore how they feel. This process should take approximately 30 seconds, then return to the sitting and the practice of mediumship.

After approximately 2 minutes I would like the student to take their focus away from the spirit communicator and to the recipient's auric field, become aware of a colour and relay to the recipient what the colour says about the recipient's character (psychic character reading).

During this process, the student should once again pause, not looking for any more information yet still being in the company of the spiritual energy (auric field) of the recipient and explore how you feel and compare your energy when working psychically as opposed to mediumistically. If there is time, I would recommend that you repeat this process two or three times during the one sitting, finishing the sitting with a message (reason for coming) from the spirit communicator.

After the sitting is completed, discuss your findings with your fellow student and compare the experiences on both the psychic and mediumistical levels and then change roles.

Exercise 7

The following exercise is designed to enhance the student's sensitivity and awareness:

It is important that this exercise does not take on the form of a competition, whereby one student is outscoring another, but the student is encouraged simply to express that of what they experience.

This exercise can be undertaken by groups of two or more students. You will require a blindfold and five plain pieces of A4 paper. Each piece of paper should be of a different colour. For many years mediums have been aware that colour emits energy, each colour vibrating at a different frequency, therefore different colours will affect people in different ways.

Decide who is going first. Beyond the student who is working, you will require a spokesperson. After the student who is working has been blindfolded, they must take time (approximately 1 minute) to settle themselves down both physically and mentally. This will allow the sensitivity to become heightened.

At this point, the spokesperson will place one of the A4 sheets of paper in the student's hands and the spokesperson will encourage the student to feel the energy that is being emitted through the colour of the paper.

The student will then, without announcing the colour they believe the paper to be, describe the experience, sensations and awareness they have of the paper.

After approximately a minute of expressing their findings, they can then announce the colour that they believe the paper to be. This process can be repeated as many times as required, each time with a different coloured paper.

Do remember, however, like all the exercises in this book, this is not a competition. It is simply a fun approach to heightening both your sensitivity and awareness.

If this exercise becomes very successful, you can replace the coloured paper with pictures. The objective being that the student who is blindfolded picks up, through their sensitivity, details of the picture.

Exercise 8

Within any act of mediumship we must accept that there will be, on one degree or another, a relationship (working partnership) between both the medium and the guide who is assisting the medium and of course, to one degree or another, some interaction between the medium and the individual communicating from the Spirit World.

Within this exercise we will look at the relationship between the guide and the medium.

The following exercise is suitable for a one-to-one environment: Put yourselves into pairs and decide between you who is going to work first. As always, it is important that the student who is working first gives him or herself time to activate and attune their mediumship. This can be best brought about, firstly, by the student having the intention that mediumship is about to take place (this mental approach will usually activate the mediumship) and secondly, allowing the mind to be passive, which will have the effect of heightening the sensitivity.

I would like the student to take his or her awareness to the recipients auric field, remembering the energy, ingredients and the make-up of the auric field comprises of energy emanating from the individuals mental, physical, emotional and spiritual states, keeping in mind that healing is about to take place.

The goal of the student is to define which aspect of the recipient would best benefit from healing. Allow yourself to become aware of the different aspects of the auric field and in your opinion, which would benefit from healing. Once this has been established I would like the student to direct his or her attention to their own guide, inviting the guide to proceed with healing for the recipient.

However, the student at this point can direct the guide as to which level (mental, physical, emotional or spiritual) they wish the healing to be directed to. I accept that usually the medium would allow the guide to direct to where the healing needs to be given, but I ask you to remember this exercise is to reinforce the working relationship between medium and guide.

Allow the healing to take place. It may be suitable at this point for some healing background music to be playing. Allow the healing to last approximately ten minutes, after which the medium can invite the guide to bring the healing to an end and for the guide to withdraw and bring the exercise to a close.

After this, the student can invite the recipient to verbalise on which level they felt they were receiving healing and compare notes. Afterwards, they can change roles.

Please remember it may be necessary that the recipient receives healing on more than just one level.

Chapter
Six

Exercises For Intermediates

Exercise 1

The first four exercises can be used individually or as a progressive collective. Suitable for one-to-one exercises, platform work or group sessions:

Put yourselves into groups of two (one-to-one sitting) and decide which student is working first.

The student who is working first will focus on the auric field of their partner (which can be found emanating approximately 2 inches from the physical body).

As the student perceives the auric field of their partner, do remember you may see, sense or hear the auric field through your sensitivity. It is important that you have in mind that you will perceive an event or subject within the auric field relating to your partner's life.

When you perceive either the subject or the event, I would like you to verbally express that which you are aware of to your partner, filling approximately 10 minutes with your findings.

The easiest way to fill the 10 minutes is to stay focused on your findings within the auric field and move your awareness further into those findings, i.e. explore in depth the information within the subject or event.

After the 10 minutes have lapsed you can bring the exercise to a close and discuss your findings, after which you can change roles, repeating the exercise.

Exercise 2

Exercise 2 is exactly the same as Exercise 1, but instead of taking 10 minutes to express your findings to your partner, you will limit this to 5 minutes, after which, you will bring your awareness away from your partner's auric field and focus on getting a link with somebody from the Spirit World who is connected in one form or another to your partner.

After you have proven survival of the individual from the Spirit World (your partner knows who the communicator is), I would like you to ask the individual in the Spirit World to give some evidence - a memory or a family story on the exact same subject that you have perceived through your partner's auric field.

This should take a further 10 minutes. Once the spirit communicator has exhausted that of which they wish to express on the chosen subject, you can bring the exercise to a close. Discuss your findings, change roles and repeat.

Exercise 3

Exercise 3 requires a set of inspirational cards. It may be advisable for you to make these cards yourself because of the subjects you want on these cards.

I would suggest approximately twenty cards. Each card will have one simple word on it, for example, holiday, vehicles, home, family, work, entertainment, education, dates, names or hobbies (one worded statements that suggest a particular subject).

These must be placed face down on a table or floor so the student who is working cannot see what is written on them. This exercise is suitable for either one-to-one sittings, platform work or group work.

Decide who is going first. The student who is working first should make a link with an individual from the Spirit World, somebody who is connected to one of your fellow students and proceed with the mediumship.

Once you have a recipient (somebody who understands the individual from the Spirit World), I would like you to pick up one of the inspirational cards whilst holding onto the company of the individual from the Spirit World, then I would like the student to invite the individual from the Spirit World to give the medium evidence, memories or family stories relating to the subject expressed on the card.

I would like the student to spend at least 5 minutes on the chosen subject, after which the student can bring the exercise to a close. Discuss your findings, change roles and repeat the exercise.

Exercise 4

Exercise 4 is very similar in its structure to Exercise 3; however, instead of finding the subject expressed through the mediumship from an inspirational card, once the student has established their link with an individual from the Spirit World and has a recipient who understands who the communicator is, I would like the student to ask the communicator for their chosen subject they wish to talk about.

Once the student working becomes aware of the subject the communicator wishes to explore, the student must verbalise to his or her recipient what the subject is the Spirit World wishes to discuss, then continue with the mediumship for approximately another 10 minutes whilst focusing on the spirit communicator's chosen subject.

When the spirit communicator has exhausted the said subject, the student can bring the exercise to a close. Discuss your findings, change roles and repeat.

Exercise 5

It is important, as an intermediate student of mediumship, that you begin to interact with those you are communicating with in the Spirit World whilst expressing your mediumship (remember the Spirit World is a world of intelligence). The following exercise is designed for this very purpose:

Decide as a group which student will work first. The student who is working first is to prepare themselves and establish a link with an individual from the Spirit World - an individual who is connected to one of the fellow students of the group.

Continue the exercise and establish your recipient to the point where your recipient understands who the communicator is. From this point on, when the student working feels that the depth of evidence and their mediumship will benefit by asking the communicator a question, they must do that very thing.

However, each time they wish to ask a question to the communicator, they must first verbalise to their recipient that they are going to ask a question. For example, let's suggest it is Grandfather who is the communicator and Grandfather is expressing that he was a builder (the word 'builder' is a general statement). The student will express the information about the building work to the recipient as long as the recipient can accept and understand the statement;

the student is to verbalise to the recipient that they are going to take their awareness back to grandfather and ask grandfather to be more specific about the nature of his work.

After the student has received more depth of information on the work, i.e. nature of work - plumber, carpenter - he or she can relay this to the recipient.

I would suggest that this is done no more than twice within the one exercise.

After you have completed the exercise, as a group, compare notes and change roles as necessary.

Exercise 6

It is important that during the practice of mediumship that you give factual information (evidence), that your recipient can both understand and accept. There is only one source where you will receive this evidence from - the spirit communicator. The following exercise will be presented as a platform exercise:

The following handout gives twelve examples of details personal to the communicator. Before the student begins to work, he or she should be encouraged to pick one of the twelve examples and during the act of mediumship the student should encourage the spirit communicator to give in-depth information (evidence) on the subject chosen.

If the student achieves their goal with ease, they can deliver a second message from the platform; however, this time, before working, pick three subjects from the list of which also have to be relayed during the second message. After completing the second message, if the student found the exercise easy, they can continue to deliver a third message from the platform; however, this time attempting to cover all the subjects on the list. This is a very mechanical way of working and I would not encourage a student to normally work in this fashion. However, we are just highlighting the potential of the limitless and varied subjects that the spirit communicator can cover during the act of mediumship.

Details Personal to the Communicator

Here are a few examples of some of the personal details an individual from the Spirit World would want to relay about himself or herself to the medium.

Physical description

Age

How they passed

Relationship to the recipient

Personality

Pastimes (Hobbies)

Memories

Places of importance

Names

Job

Anniversaries

It is important to remember when working with the World of Spirit that, as mediums, we allow the information to be relayed to us in a natural manner and that the interaction between the communicator and the medium does not become too mechanical.

Exercise 7

It is important that during the act of mediumship that the medium expresses both the evidence and indeed the presence of Spirit to the communicator (what I mean by the presence of Spirit is that the recipient cannot only accept the factual evidence but can also feel the company of their loved one from the Spirit World through the mediumship of the student who is working).

The following exercise is designed to bring this about. It is best suited as a one-to-one exercise but can be expressed from the platform or indeed a group environment:

Put yourselves into pairs and decide who is working first. The student who is working first should prepare themselves to work and establish a link with an individual from the Spirit World - somebody who is connected to the recipient.

Spend 5 minutes giving evidence from the individual from the Spirit World, after which, I would like the student who is working to stop looking for further evidence, sit in the quiet with the company of the spirit communicator, inviting the spirit communicator to draw ever closer, with the purpose of allowing the communicator to be in the company of their loved one, i.e. the recipient, for no other purpose than the beauty of being in the loved one's company.

Immediately, before going into the quiet, the student who is working must announce to their recipient what they are about to do and what their intentions are. After 2 minutes of sitting in the quiet and allowing your recipient to have the company of their loved one, then begin to interact with the communicator once again, with the goal of giving the message (reason for coming) and then bring the sitting to a close.

After this, the student should invite the recipient to voice what he or she felt - did they feel the company of their loved one or not? Then, change roles and repeat the exercise.

Exercise 8

Remembering that the Spirit World is a world of intelligence, there are times when a spirit communicator will express their presence through emotions. This can sometimes be challenging for students. However, information such as emotion is nothing more than spiritual energy and if as a student you can have this approach to emotions, they will only add and bring depth to your mediumship.

The following exercise is designed with emotions in mind, ideal from the platform or as a one-to-one sitting exercise:

As a platform exercise, the individual working must prepare themselves and establish a link with an individual from the Spirit World, verbalise their findings and establish a recipient.

Once your recipient is comfortable that they know who the communicator is, I would like the student to invite the communicator to express some evidence and emotions referring to something that has happened within the family of the recipient since the communicator has gone to the Spirit World.

Firstly, this will simply be expressed as an emotion. The student working must express the emotion to the recipient. The emotion must be immediately followed by factual information from the communicator about the incident, memory or event within the recipient's family to support the initial emotions.

As long as the recipient can understand both the emotions and the factual information supporting the emotions, the student who is working can bring the mediumship to a close and discuss their findings.

If at any time the student finds the emotions overpowering, simply, through the power of your mind, detach yourself from the emotions yet still express them. Remember you are in control of the energy, the energy is not in control of you.

Exercise 9

This exercise is designed with remote viewing in mind. Remote viewing is a form of mediumship whereby the medium will move his or her awareness through a chosen location of importance offered up by the communicator from the Spirit World. For example, the communicator may show you his home and the medium may first become aware of the living room and through the student's awareness the medium will journey from the living room to the next room and can indeed mediumistically journey through the whole of the house, describing to the recipient what they see and are aware of and indeed the layout of the house as they journey through it.

This exercise is suitable for both the platform and as a one-to-one sitting:

Decide who is going first and give the student who is about to work time to attune themselves to the exercise ahead. I would like the student to invite and become aware of the company of an individual from the Spirit World, an individual who connects in one form or another to someone else in the group.

Begin to verbalise what you are aware of (male/female, loose description, how the communicator is related to the recipient) until you have a recipient who understands who the communicator is. This part of the exercise should take approximately 5 minutes.

After this, through the power of your mind, the student who is working will ask the communicator to show them a location of importance. Once the student becomes aware of the location, I would like them to take their awareness and journey through the location, verbalising their experience to the recipient as they do so. As long as the recipient understands the location, the student can then go on to giving the reason for coming (the message) from the communicator and then bring the sitting to an end. Discuss your findings and change roles.

It is important that the student has in mind at all times, whilst working, that the location offered up from the spirit communicator is the communicator's choice and not the student's. I would recommend you practise this exercise both as a one-to-one sitting and from the platform.

If you are comfortable with this exercise, repeat. However, on the second run through, ask the communicator to give you *two* locations of importance. With your awareness, journey through and describe the first location and then, through the power of your mediumship, journey whilst describing the journey to your recipient, from the first location to the second location. Then, journey through and describe the second location.

Exercise 10

The following exercise is designed to allow the recipient to feel the presence of their loved one who is communicating from the spirit side of life.

This exercise is suitable for both one-to-one sittings and to be demonstrated from the platform.

After the student who is working has given themselves time and space to activate and attune their mediumship, I would like them to proceed with a regular one-to-one sitting, giving evidence and information to the recipient about the individual who is communicating from the Spirit World.

I would like this process to take approximately 10 minutes. Once your recipient is comfortable that they know who the communicator is, I would like the medium to begin to give the message (reason for coming). However, during this aspect of the sitting, preferably once, for approximately 1 minute when suitable, I would like the medium to verbalise as the loved one from the Spirit World; for example, if the communicator was expressing their support to the recipient because they were going through a challenging time in their life, the medium may say something to the effect of: "Your mother is expressing her support for you from the Spirit World at this time", where in this exercise the medium would verbalise it as the following: "I'm giving you my support at this time" (words and thoughts directly from the mother, the medium verbalising as the mother).

This has a psychological effect upon the medium, which in turn brings about the wonderful phenomena of encouraging the communicator to blend even closer with the medium, i.e. stepping closer to the recipient, which brings about the desired effect of allowing the recipient to feel the presence of the communicator, for example, their mother.

Following this, I would like the medium to bring the sitting to an end, remembering how the communicator wishes to end the sitting, not how the medium wishes to end the sitting. On completing the exercise, you can discuss your findings (did the recipient feel the presence of their loved one during the sitting?) and then change roles.

Please remember, there are many different types of evidence. If your client can feel or is aware of their loved one from the Spirit World, can I suggest that this is spiritual evidence.

Chapter
Seven

Exercises For
The Advanced

Exercise 1

It is important that we accept that when the spirit communicator is interacting with the medium and expressing information, that they are communicating through their own intelligence. Therefore, logic tells us there would not be one worded statements, for example, the medium expressing the information as follows: "You could take the name **JOHN**, you would understand the connection with **BIRMINGHAM** and you would understand a **CARPENTER**," when in fact what the spirit communicator has relayed to the medium is: "My name is John, I lived in Birmingham and I was a carpenter."

Evidence is an expression of the intelligence of Spirit. Therefore, as the first example shows, random one worded statements at best can only be information, yet when a statement expressed by the medium that gives information supported by further information that tells a full story and can be accepted by the recipient as equal evidence.

The following exercises will encourage the medium during the act of mediumship to be aware of where there is depth within a statement from the Spirit World. For example, evidence:

Put yourselves into groups of three. Every member of the group in turn will have a turn at being the medium, so at any given time you will have a medium, a recipient and an observer. When the medium is working, he or she has the option of going directly to a recipient to establish who indeed is the recipient and who is the observer, or the medium can put the evidence out to both people in the group and very quickly, through the information and evidence, it will become apparent who is the recipient and therefore who is the observer.

Now, the observer's job is a very important part of the exercise; it is the observer's job whilst the medium is working through their own mediumship and sensitivity to observe the energy of the medium to establish where the medium can go back into the energy of a statement they have just made to enrich the statement, i.e. turning a statement from information into evidence.

I would like the observer in any given exercise to advise the medium to go back into the information of a statement they have just made with a goal to enrich it no more than three times throughout the duration of the exercise and only after the recipient has said "yes" to the initial statement, for example, if a medium was to express to a recipient: "Your father's making me aware he passed with a chest condition" and the recipient replayed "yes" to this statement.

As an observer, as long as the energy within the exercise was good enough with the medium to go back to enrich that statement, I would ask them to do so.

For example, when the medium takes their awareness back to the information, the probability is they will become aware of what type of chest condition Father died of, i.e. heart attack, lung disease, pneumonia.

On expressing the information for a second time, yet now with depth of information, the medium turns the information into evidence.

I would suggest each sitting should take approximately 15 to 20 minutes. After each sitting I would like the group of three to discuss the mechanics of the individual sitting; how difficult or natural was it for the medium to go back into the energy to gather even more information and how on doing so it enriched the recipient's sitting?

At no time during this exercise should the observer direct the medium to go back looking for specific information, but, instead, a simple phrase such as: "Can you go back into that previous information within mind to enrich it?" would be sufficient.

Repeat exercise so every individual within the group can experience being the medium.

Exercise 2

Exercise 2 is only an extension of Exercise 1.

Put yourselves into groups of two, so this time we have removed the observer, leaving the medium and the recipient. Proceed with a sitting. During the sitting I would like the medium to verbalise to the recipient minimal once, maximum three times, when they are going to go back into the energy of a statement they have just made to the recipient, within mind to enrich that statement with further information i.e. turning information into evidence.

Just as before, I would suggest the exercise take approximately 15 to 20 minutes.

On completion, take time to discuss your findings and then change roles and repeat the exercise.

Exercise 3

Exercise 3 is an extension of Exercises 1 and 2.

Again, put yourselves into pairs and proceed with a sitting. But this time, although I would like the medium to be actively, when the energy is right for it, going back into the information with a goal of enriching the evidence with further information, I do not want the medium to tell the recipient when they are doing this, allowing it to be more natural.

Again, I would recommend 15 to 20 minutes for each sitting. However, at the end of each sitting, I would like the medium to tell the recipient when they have gone back and how natural they found it to put into practice and the recipient to tell the medium because of the depth of evidence, how, if at all, it enriched their sitting.

These exercises can be carried out as three progressive exercises or individual exercises.

Exercise 4

It is important during the act of mediumship that we encourage ourselves to be factual with the statements we offer up to the recipient. So the following exercise will encourage students to be more factual within their work:

This exercise is suitable for group work:

Place the chairs in two circles, an inner circle and an outer circle with the chairs facing each other so the inner circle is facing the outer circle and vice-versa, positioned for one-to-one sittings but to form a circle. Whilst being in one large circle, you are working in pairs. Those students on the inner circle will be the mediums first.

The medium's goal is not to give a structured sitting to their recipient but, instead, to prove the person you have with you from the Spirit World in as fewer statements as possible. This requires the medium to be full, clear, concise and factual with their statements.

The medium is allowed to express no more than six statements. During this sitting it is the recipient's job to verbalise to the medium how many statements the medium has made at any given time, remembering that the medium has a limit of six statements.

Once the medium has exhausted the six statements he or she must stop working, immaterial of whether the recipient knows who the communicator is or not; however, once the recipient knows who the communicator is, be it after one statement or six, the recipient must raise their hand in the air, indicating that they know who the communicator is.

At this point, all verbalisation between the medium and the recipient must cease. This process must take a maximum of 5 minutes. As soon as the 5 minutes have lapsed, the mediums seated on the inner circle must all stand and move to the neighbouring chair clockwise whilst the students on the outer circle stay seated as they were. The mediums, now finding themselves in a new chair facing a new recipient, must repeat the exercise, remembering no more than six statements, no more than 5 minutes, equally remembering the recipient's job to verbalise the number of statements and to raise their hands when they know who the communicator is.

This exercise must be repeated four times, after which the recipients and mediums change roles and repeat.

The exercise will encourage students to be more precise and full in their individual statements that they offer up to their clients.

Exercise 5

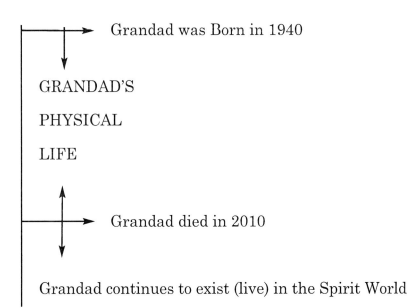

Grandad was Born in 1940

GRANDAD'S

PHYSICAL

LIFE

Grandad died in 2010

Grandad continues to exist (live) in the Spirit World

Mediums can sometimes be guilty during a message, or sitting, of limiting themselves to information based around the latter part of a communicator's life, i.e. illness and death, yet if we look at the example given above, we will see that Grandad was 70 when he died, therefore he has 70 years of knowledge, experiences and stories to tell, so the following exercise will encourage the student to give a fuller life story (memories) of the communicator:

This exercise will take the form of a one-to-one sitting or could equally be done as a platform exercise.

Put yourselves into pairs and decide who initially will be the medium and who will be the recipient. The medium can proceed to give a sitting. Once the recipient and only when the recipient knows who the communicator is, I would like the medium to ask the communicator to give some information (memories or evidence) of at least two different eras from their life.

When and only when this has been accepted, then I would like the medium to ask the communicator to give some evidence of something that has happened within the family on the Earth plane since they have been in the Spirit World. This can be followed by a message (reason for coming) and the closing of the sitting.

Swapping roles, you can then repeat the exercise. I would suggest 20 minutes for each exercise. This exercise will encourage the medium to give a fuller and more in-depth picture of the communicator's life as a whole.

Exercise 6

If the Spirit World can express their intelligence then surely the Spirit World can express their emotions. Emotions on their own are not evidential, but if they come with the reason behind the emotion they can become evidence.

This exercise is suitable for either platform work or a one-to-one sitting:

Put yourselves into pairs and decide between yourselves who will be the medium first and who will be the medium second. I would like the medium to proceed to give the recipient a sitting. When and only when the recipient understands who the communicator is, I would like the medium to ask the communicator to express an emotion relating to something the communicator has observed from the Spirit World within their family on the Earth plane.

Allow your mind to be still, thus allowing yourself to submerge within the emotion. This will allow the energy of the emotion to be expressed through your mediumship to your recipient to the point where your recipient will feel the emotion.

The medium, at this point, must verbalise to their client what emotion they are feeling. The client, at this point, if they wish to, can express if they can feel the emotion. Then I would like the medium to ask the communicator to give them some evidence behind the emotion, such as some factual information as to why they are expressing that emotion, which will allow the emotion supported by the information to bring about evidence, then follow this with a message (reason for coming).

Then bring the sitting or demonstration to an end, after which I would like both medium and recipient to discuss the effect the emotion had upon the mediumship.

Did it empower the mediumship?

Take away from the mediumship?

Was the medium comfortable within the energy of emotion?

After this, both students can change roles and repeat the exercise. I would suggest approximately 20 minutes for each exercise.

Exercise 7

It is important at all times when a student is working that they are both managing and in control of his or her energy and in control and managing the interaction and relationship with the Spirit World.

The following exercise will help to bring this about. This is an exercise suitable for both one-to-one sittings and platform work:

After attuning themselves, the student can take to the platform and proceed to present his or her mediumship in the form of a demonstration, just giving one message.

Once the medium has a recipient and established the continuity of life, i.e. the recipient knows who the medium has from the Spirit World, I would like the student to ask the communicator to go back to the Spirit World and to bring back with them, to the company, a second communicator who the same recipient would understand.

Once the medium becomes aware now of both communicators, I would like the medium to ask the first communicator to step back (yet not to go back to the Spirit World but to just step back to the perimeter of the medium's awareness) and at this point I would like the medium to focus solely on the second communicator. Once the second communicator has been established and accepted by the recipient,

I would like the medium to invite the second communicator to step away and indeed to return to the Spirit World.

At this point, the medium would invite the first communicator to step forward again, whereby in the company of the first communicator, the medium will offer up the message (reason for coming) to the recipient and bring it to an end.

Exercise 8

This exercise is suitable for group sessions. Decide between yourselves who will go first. The student will proceed by establishing a link with an individual in the Spirit World and giving off the information.

Once the medium has established a recipient and the recipient is comfortable they know who the communicator is, I would like the medium to ask the communicator to step to one side, at this point inviting a second communicator from the Spirit World to step forward.

Within the medium's mind, they must accept that the second communicator will have no connection to the first communicator and indeed be for a different recipient and proceed to give evidence and information relating to the second communicator.

When the medium has a recipient who is comfortable that they know who the communicator is, the medium can ask the second communicator to step back and for the first communicator once again to step forward. The medium, at this point, turning their focus to the first recipient, giving one or two more pieces of evidence followed by a message (reason for coming) should bring this first message to an end, inviting the first communicator to withdraw and return to the Spirit World, at the same time inviting the second communicator to step forward.

At this point, the medium takes his or her attention to the remaining recipient, giving one or two pieces of evidence which will re-establish the link with the second communicator, followed by the message (reason for coming) and bring both the message and the exercise to a close.

This exercise should take approximately 10 minutes, after which discuss your findings with the group.

The key to this exercise is whilst the medium is in the company of two communicators, it is important that the medium keeps both communicators separate at all times during the duration of the exercise

Exercise 9

As an advanced student of mediumship it is important to find different ways to maximise, enrich and enhance the energy (fuel) in which we work. One of the ways we can do this is by allowing the communicator to talk about or express something they are or were when on the Earth plane or passionate about, i.e. their job, family, sport or indeed hobby.

The following exercise is suited for a one-to-one exercise:

Once you have decided who is going first, the student who is working should take time to prepare and attune him or herself to the Spirit World. During this time I would like the student to send out thoughts to the Spirit World that as an individual steps forward from the Spirit World they express in depth something they are passionate about.

Therefore, the format of the sitting will be no more than the medium expressing very little about the communicator other than male or female, young or old, family or non-family, followed by the majority of the sitting, with information on the activity of that the communicator was passionate about.

Through this information and only through this information, the recipient understands who the communicator is, then the medium can give the message (reason for coming) and then bring it to an end, after which the students can change roles and repeat the exercise.

The student working is looking for the passion of the communicator to fuel and enhance the mediumship. After both students have worked, you can discuss your findings. Both students should work for approximately 20 minutes.

Exercise 10

As advanced students of mediumship it is important that we have the ability to be able to read the quality of energy of what we are working in at any given time, thus knowing when we can enrich the information with further information, or alternatively and equally important, knowing when we have exhausted a particular pocket of information and when to move on to the next pocket of information.

This exercise is suitable for two students working within the same energy (a double link) on the platform:

Before proceeding, the two students must decide who will be medium number 1 and who will be medium number 2. Medium number 1 must establish the link with the Spirit World and proceed to carry out the mediumship. At all times medium number 2 must have in their mind that they are staying within the energy and the space of medium number 1, which will allow them to become aware of the spirit communicator who is communicating with medium number 1.

As medium number 1 proceeds with the mediumship, if medium number 2 feels that any statements (evidence) made by medium number 1 have scope for improvement through depth of information, medium number 2 will take their awareness to the communicator and invite the communicator to give more information on the previous statement that medium number 1 has just made to the recipient.

After this, medium number 2 will intervene and verbalise their findings to the recipient, i.e. adding to the evidence. This must be done minimum once, maximum three times throughout the duration of the exercise, after which medium number 1 can give the message (reason for coming) and bring the exercise to an end.

This exercise should take 10 to 12 minutes.

Do discuss your findings.

Exercise 11

It is important that advanced students of mediumship become comfortable during the practice of mediumship that they bring depth and structure and allow themselves to work the evidence. The following exercise is one way of catering for this. This exercise is suitable as a platform demonstrating exercise or a one-to-one sitting exercise. I will present it to you as a platform exercise:

The student prepares (attunes) themselves and from the platform begins to present their mediumship. The goal of the exercise is, that once the student establishes a recipient, they invite the spirit communicator to present two completely different pieces of evidence; each piece of evidence containing the same word, but with different meanings (homophones).

For example: "For an elderly lady, your grandmother was a very active lady and was really careful with her diet and would have at least one *orange* a day for its vitamin c. Sadly, she thought that she was healthier than she actually was and took it upon herself to decorate her home, one of the rooms she painted *orange*. Shortly after, sadly she had a heart attack and passed away."

Another example is: "Your grandfather was a keen gardener and at the bottom of the garden was a *pear* tree and to get into the garden you had to go through a conservatory and for many years after Grandfather passed there was a *pair* of his wellington boots left in the conservatory that nobody wanted to move due to the emotional connection to them."

Now, the pitfall of this exercise is that the student overthinks the exercise whilst doing it and formats the homophones in their own mind. It is important that the student allows the communicator from the Spirit World to express the homophones through their intelligence and not the students. On completing the goal, the student can move onto the message (reason for coming) and then bring the mediumship to a close.

Again, the exercise can be repeated according to how many students within the group and timings available.

Exercise 12

I would like you to organise an exercise that involves remote viewing as explained in a previous exercise, either as a one-to-one exercise or expressed from the platform.

Begin the exercise to the point where the student both has a recipient and the recipient understands who the communicator is. This should have taken approximately 10 minutes to this point, after which, I would like the student, through the power of their mediumship, to ask the communicator to express and show a location of importance from their past.

I would like the student to move their awareness, i.e. journey through the location, verbalising that that they experienced and see to the recipient as they do so. Once the recipient is comfortable that they know if the location that the communicator is referring to then I would like the student to ask the communicator to express a second location, this time a location connected to the recipient and repeat the remote viewing.

Remember, the World of Spirit is a world of intelligence and the communicator will show locations that are relevant to the message: for example, the communicator may show the location of their workplace when they were on the Earth plane followed by the location of the workplace of the recipient, simply because they wish to talk about the recipient's work.

Once you have achieved and your recipient understands both locations, this can be followed by the message (reason for coming).

It is possible that the message, in one form or another, will relate to the remote viewing. This must at all times be directed by the spirit communicator.

After the message you can bring the sitting to an end. Discuss your findings and change roles.

Exercise 13

Within the following exercise, we return to the exercise that has already been expressed as an intermediate exercise, whereby the medium verbalises as the communicator, yet this time we format the exercise on an advanced level.

As always, this exercise is suitable for both platform and one-to-one sittings.

If we format the exercise as a one-to-one sitting, you can adjust the exercise to suit the platform as and when necessary.

Put yourselves into pairs and decide which student will work first, after which, allow the student who is working the space and time to activate and attune their mediumship. Proceed with a regular sitting, bringing information and evidence from a communicator. Only when your recipient understands who the communicator is and after approximately 10 minutes has lapsed, I would like you, the medium, to invite your recipient to put a question to the communicator from the Spirit World.

So as to avoid the medium's mind becoming too involved, I would ask the recipient not to put a question that can only be answered with a factual answer. For example, can you tell me the town/city you were born in? This can only be answered from the Spirit World with an answer such as:

London/Liverpool. If the recipient could pose a more general question, for example, if the recipient was thinking of selling their home and relocating, the recipient may pose the question: What do you think of my plans with the house? This will give scope for the communicator to give a more in-depth, yet not necessarily, factual answer.

The answer in its entirety must be offered up from the medium to the recipient verbally, as if it was the communicator saying it themself. A word of warning at this point, it is important that the medium does not try to be overly factual with the answer, but allows themself to be inspired from the communicator with the answer. After the answer has been completed, the medium can proceed to the reason for coming (the message) and then bring the sitting to an end. This exercise will be approximately 20 minutes in its entirety. After this, compare notes (don't be surprised that although the medium during the answer was not trying to be factual, from the recipients point of view it may indeed be very relevant) and change roles.

Chapter
Eight

Closing
Thoughts

The development of mediumship should never be undertaken lightly. Mediumistical development should unfold in harmony with spiritual development, that is to say when developing one's mediumship one should be developing oneself.

Please remember the act of mediumship is an act of service to the Spirit World and to Mankind. Our goals as mediums should be to prove the continuity of life through the act of mediumship and to bring spiritual comfort and upliftment to the recipient.

Through the exercises in this book, we have looked at how we can enrich our mediumship, but I ask you to give some thought as to how you can enrich your spiritual wellbeing. One suggestion would be through the practice of meditation, something this book has not touched upon.

I can only encourage and promote those of you who are developing your mediumship to meditate because of the values and positive abilities that meditation will bring to each you, your spirituality and your mediumship. Maybe a subject we can cover in more depth in the next book...

Books and CDs I would like to recommend for your reading and education are:

'How To Be A Medium' by W.H. Evans

'The Unseen Self: Kirlian Photography Explained' by Brian Snellgrove

'The University of Spiritualism' by Harry Boddington

Also check out the meditational CDs by Libby Clark OSNU and also of Shelia French DSNU